I0809853

THEN & NOW

CARROLLTON

OPPOSITE: The Carrollton Motor Car Company was once a prominent part of downtown Carrollton. Taken around 1920, this is a photograph of the company's tow truck. The location was later a Chevrolet dealership and is now home to Myers Tin Shop. (Courtesy of Dick Griffin.)

THEN & NOW

CARROLLTON

Janice Van Horne-Lane

For Dr. George E. and Helen Rankin and Velma Griffin
—thanks for paving the way.

ISBN 978-0-7385-7785-2

Library of Congress Control Number: 2009932622

Published by Arcadia Publishing
Charleston SC, Chicago IL, Portsmouth NH, San Francisco CA

Printed in the United States of America

For all general information contact Arcadia Publishing at:
Telephone 843-853-2070
Fax 843-853-0044
E-mail sales@arcadiapublishing.com
For customer service and orders:
Toll-Free 1-888-313-2665

Visit us on the Internet at www.arcadiapublishing.com

On the Front Cover: Ben Franklin is one of the longest continually operating stores in Carrollton. John and Evelyn Ashton opened this store just five days after they were married. A museum has opened in their honor at their former home on Third Street NW. Two doors are visible in the historic photograph—at one time patrons had to go out one side and enter the other to view the entire store. (Then photograph courtesy of Dick Griffin; now photograph courtesy of Nicole K. Taggart.)

On the Back Cover: The Union School sat on Second Street NE and was replaced by the current elementary building in 1913. These are some of the children from the Union School days. (Courtesy of Dick Griffin)

Contents

Acknowledgments

I am always amazed and delighted at the help given me when I announce I am working on a local history project. Without the help of neighbors, friends, and family, a work like this would be virtually impossible. I truly thank everyone who helped bring this book to light for their encouragement, their memories, and their use of photographs.

The body of this book is, of course, the historical photographs. A special thanks goes to John and Susan Rutledge for allowing me to once again use Dr. George E. Rankin's pictures. Thanks also go to Dick Griffin for the use of his collection and to the Carroll County Historical Society and John Davis for their help in seeing this through to completion and for their photographs as well.

A special thanks goes to those who helped in identifying specific locations. I thank the Jobes family for their help in identifying the stores that once were their neighbors, Joel Rogers and Mike Ulman for helping figure out the Napa building, and Vickie Nign for the old *Free Press Standard* buildings. I also thank Vickie Nign for her photographs of Carrollton Graphics and Al's IGA. Great thanks also go to the Carroll County Genealogical Library for some of their old photographs as well. I would still be at a loss for the Ellen Owen house if not for Amber Grunder and Jean Scarlott. Thanks ladies! I also want to thank Dan Ries for his wonderful postcard collection.

The modern photographs proved to be more of a challenge than I had anticipated. It was with a huge thanks to Nicole K. Taggart that these photographs were obtained. Unless otherwise noted, Nicole took all the now photographs. I hope the sunburn and sore feet were worth it. It is with a huge hug and thanks to my dad, E. Leroy Van Horne (Carroll County auditor), that the courthouse photographs were obtained. He was the brave soul who was able to go to the top of the courthouse tower and take the beautiful aerial views of our town. I only wish I could have shared them all with you; maybe in another work. I also thank Richard Lewis and Julia Incerpi for their willingness to pose outside of Ben Franklin for the cover photograph.

Last, but not least, thanks to my family for their patience while I locked myself away in the office to work while they paced impatiently outside for their meals. I love you!

Introduction

Someone once asked me what it was like to live my whole life in a small town. The question took me by surprise, and I did not know how to answer. I had lived a few other places while in college and when I first married, but Carrollton has been my home for nearly 40 years. I have thought about that question for some time, and the only response I can give is "security."

There is a security in being in a place where nearly everyone knows who you are. You feel safe knowing you can still borrow a cup of sugar from your neighbors. Grocery stores and gas stations may not be open 24 hours a day. Banks still close at noon on Wednesday and Saturday, and there is a certain Mayberry quality to the whole thing. But there is a security in all that.

Carrollton is a small town in northeastern Ohio that has no major claims to fame except being named the safest rural place to live. During the Civil War, Carrollton had the fighting McCooks, John Hunt Morgan's raid, and John McTammany. The Underground Railroad had stops throughout the countryside. Cy Young once played baseball here, and it has been rumored that Ted Healy, creator of the Three Stooges, lived here for a time (but that has yet to be proven). In more recent years, Kirk Lowdermilk put Carrollton on the map by playing professional football for the Minnesota Vikings. Several others have gone on to other locations and done great things, but no presidents or famous actors or have ever lived here.

However, it is not any specific individual but the group of people who live here that makes Carrollton unique. In October 2008, Carrollton was named by the *Progressive Farmer* as the safest rural community in the United States with the lowest crime rate in the nation. Some would say it is because there is nothing to do here, but I believe it is because this is a small town where everyone knows somebody, so if you do something wrong, your chances of getting caught are pretty high. Many residents have lived in Carrollton most of their lives, and, in a sense, it is more like a big family. That is why the residents care so much about the surroundings. If a building has to come down, the entire family mourns its loss. I write this book in memory of all the buildings we have lost and to all those still standing, so if one day they too have to be removed, future generations will look back with the fond memories we, the current generation, have. Then, hopefully, they will add their own memories to these pages.

These memories have accrued since the town was first settled in 1800, and it is only right that they continue to do so. When Peter Bohart founded this village as Centreville in 1815, and then Isaac Atkinson helped develop a new county and changed the name to Carrollton in 1833, I doubt they ever dreamed their names would still be on the tongues of generations 200 years later. I feel it is only right to continue their story by sharing it with you.

I hope you will take some time to sit with a younger person in your life and flip through these pages and share your memories while making new ones. We have so much to treasure and value that I only wish there were more pages to fit it all in. Perhaps there will be more books in the future to help preserve all the memories of each of Carroll County's towns and places.

CHAPTER 1

Where It All Began on the Public Square

One of the most recognizable places in Carrollton is the Public Square, which has seen many changes over the years. In 1814, Peter Bohart built a tavern at the crossroads on the north end for travelers coming from Steubenville, Lisbon, Canton, and New Philadelphia. This is a view looking south from North Lisbon taken in the early 1900s. (Courtesy of the Carroll County Historical Society.)

Two years before platting the town of Centreville, Peter Bohart constructed this house (shown below) as a tavern, and it is probably the oldest building still standing in Carrollton. Its original site was on the corner of East Main and North Lisbon Streets (the northeast corner of Public Square). At the end of the Civil War, it was purchased by Sheriff John Hemming and was moved to its current location at 256 Second Street NE. (Courtesy of the Carroll County Historical Society.)

This corner has certainly changed since Bohart's Tavern sat here. Once the tavern was moved, Samuel M. "Doc" Stockon had the current building constructed in 1876. The ground floor housed the Stockon Bank, the Samuel Stockon Drug Store, and the medical office of Samuel's brother, Dr. Leander Stockon. The bank portion remained a bank through successive ownership until the late 1990s, when Carroll County commissioners purchased the building. It now houses the Ohio Bureau of Support. (Courtesy of the Carroll County Genealogical Society.)

This building was erected in 1841 by Henry A. Stidger at a cost of 37.5¢ per day for the brickwork. It was billed as "the Store in the Hollow" and was especially known for its ballroom on the third floor, which served for a time as the Carrollton Academy. It was here that John McTammany manufactured his player pianos and created the punch card voting system. Since the early 1990s, it has been an antique store called Trunks and Treasures. (Courtesy of the author.)

Below is the east side of the square. The building in the foreground was constructed around 1815 as a private home and was later run as a hotel by various owners. In 1877, it became the Aldridge Hotel, and in 1892, it was sold to Mr. and Mrs. Elias Fisher, who called it the Commercial Hotel. In 1907, it became the Park Hotel. In 1996, the building was razed, and the lot has since been used as parking for courthouse employees. (Courtesy of the Carroll County Historical Society.)

The original courthouse was built in 1835 on land donated by Isaac Atkinson, an Ohio state representative who promoted the formation of Carroll County. It stood about where the lampposts are in the current photograph (above) and was used until 1884, when the second floor began to sink. A new courthouse was built in 1885, with the cornerstone being laid on May 22, and it was officially dedicated on September 29, 1886, by former governor George Hoadly. (Courtesy of the Rankin family.)

The first known jail sat on Liberty Street (now Third Street SE) and then moved to a house just east of the courthouse. In 1974, that building was razed, and the current jail was erected at 43 Second Street SE. The jail is attached to the courthouse and serves as its main entrance. The county commissioners and sheriff have their offices here. (Courtesy of the Rankin family.)

This was the site of the county treasurer's office until 1895, when Mrs. L. V. H. Baker and her sister opened a general store. The store was on the first floor, and Mrs. Baker lived on the second. The Masonic Chapter, the Blue Lodge, and the Order of Eastern Star occupied the third floor. George Butler had a store in this location, and later it was used by the J. C. Penney Company. Today it is the location of the local Internet café. (Courtesy of Dick Griffin.)

In 1837, Daniel McCook built this large home (below) for his family with bricks made just at the other end of the block. He fought during the Civil War along with eight of his sons and six of his nephews. George Butler later purchased the house and used it as a storefront. It is now owned by the Ohio Historical Society and is operated by the Carroll County Historical Society as a museum. (Courtesy of the Carroll County Genealogical Society.)

The west side of Public Square has changed over the years. Below, the building in the foreground is McFadden's Insurance, and the Van Horn building is visible in the background. The buildings in the older image were photographed just after a fire. When they were replaced, a barbershop and bowling alley were established in the basement of the new building. Sadly, those doorways were closed off in 2003 when new sidewalks were poured. Dotty's Crafts and Archer's Restaurant are now in this location. (Courtesy of the Rankin family.)

McLaughlin's store was a tobacco shop that sold a little bit of everything. It was built in 1908 and stood on the northwest corner of the square. The land was purchased in 1919 and the building subsequently razed by J. P. Cummings for the construction of Cummings Bank. The building has been a bank ever since and today is the location of National City Bank, a branch of PNC. (Courtesy of the Rankin family.)

This building was only two stories tall when it was constructed by James Sinclair in 1829. Daniel Van Horn added the third floor when he purchased the building in 1867. The upper two floors are now empty. McCort's is just one of the businesses on the ground level. The corner (now a jewelry store) was once home to the Cummings Bank and later was the City Meat Market. The Carroll County Visitor's Bureau is located in an office in the back. (Courtesy of the Carroll County Historical Society.)

CHAPTER 2

MAIN STREET OR OAK HILL

The hub of most business districts is Main Street. Carrollton's Main Street runs east and west, and parts are also state routes, such as 9, 39, and 43. This photograph of Main Street was taken around 1909. A portion of the west half was once called Oak Hill, and the eastern side was known as Sheep Hill. (Courtesy of the Carroll County Historical Society.)

This view is of East Main Street taken from the top of the courthouse. The older photograph was taken before 1913, because the elementary school, which was constructed then, is absent from the view. The building that houses the current One Way Youth center is visible in both photographs. The buildings in the foreground of the current photograph now house the Ohio Department of Jobs and Family Services. The modern view also shows Overlook Lane on the outskirts of town, which was once merely a field. (Then photograph courtesy of the Rankin family; now photograph courtesy of E. Leroy Van Horne.)

East Main Street was once called "Gasoline Alley," because there were numerous car dealerships and gas stations in a two-block stretch. The building in the foreground was a Maytag dealer and an IGA grocery store. The building labeled MK Market is now home to the *Free Press Standard* offices. At an early time, it was part of the Carrollton Motor Car Company. (Courtesy of the Rankin family.)

The Dairy Isle was built by Mac McClelland around 1956. Some time in the late 1960s, an indoor eating area was added. It later became Graber's Restaurant and then a pizza parlor. In the mid-1990s, it was transformed into a doctor's office and was most recently home to the General Education Development offices. Now the building sits empty. (Courtesy of Vickie Nign.)

One of the more recognizable homes in Carrollton was built around 1900 by A. E. Albright on the corner of East Main Street and McCook Avenue. Albright owned and operated the Albright China Company, which thrived until the Great Depression hit. He was then forced to sell the business and his home. Today the home is divided into apartments. (Courtesy of the Rankin family.)

A. E. and Tillie Albright built the tabernacle directly behind their home in 1905 to be used for interdenominational gatherings. It was mainly used for this purpose until 1944, when it was purchased by the Wesley Community Chapel. They occupied the building until a new church was constructed on Twelfth Street in the early 1980s. In 1915, it served as a temporary school building while the elementary school was being built. In the 1990s, the building was purchased for use as the One Way Youth Center. (Courtesy of the Rankin family.)

Jones's Sunoco sat adjacent to the Albright property and was part of "Gasoline Alley" for many years. It was purchased by Ray Jones in 1955, and he sold it around 1980. Some time after that it was sold again and became SS&E laundry service, which provides laundry services for the Carroll Health Care Center. The above picture was taken around 1965. The last gas station on this section of Main Street closed in 2008. (Courtesy of Vickie Nign.)

The Jerusalem (or Reformed) Church began in 1832, when members began meeting in the home of A. E. and Tillie Albright. On June 16, 1847, the cornerstone was laid to begin construction on this building, located at the corner of East Main Street and Park Avenue. It is not certain when the spires were removed. Today the sign on the door reads "The Historical Baptist Church." (Courtesy of the author.)

R. E. Miller's Car Company is still a part of Carson's Napa Store. It faces Park Avenue and is used for storing various parts for cars, trucks, and other motor vehicles. A newer garage was built on the corner of Main Street and Park Avenue and sells parts from the Napa distribution center on Lincoln Avenue next to the Carrollton Baptist Temple. The bright blue paint on this building makes it stand out. (Courtesy of Dick Griffin.)

The Carrollton Motor Car Company was once located at 44 East Main Street and sold L&M Rubber tires, which were manufactured in Carrollton. Today it is the site of Myers Tin Shop, which is owned and operated by Jim Myers. The tin shop was previously located on North Lisbon Street, and its former building can be seen on page 61. (Courtesy of Jim Myers.)

Turning the corner from the square and heading along Main Street, the side of the bank building, Dr. Pearch's former office, Bud's Farm Toys, and the Virginia Restaurant and Lounge are visible. The Virginia Restaurant and Lounge was the third brick structure built in Carrollton and has had many names and owners. One of its owners was Daniel Van Horn before he purchased the building on the opposite corner. The Virginia Restaurant and Lounge has also been called Hoopes House and the Colonial. (Courtesy of the author.)

Once the site of the *Free Press Standard* offices, Sporting Goods, a taxi service, and Peacock Cleaners (later McFadden's Insurance), these buildings were razed in 1974 to create a much-needed public parking area. The lot is called Municipal Parking and, until the mid-1980s, was the only public parking lot in downtown Carrollton. It is one of the only parking lots in America that still uses penny parking meters. Customers can park for 12 minutes per penny. (Courtesy of the Rankin family.)

The western end of Municipal Parking was the site of Swan's Electric, which was owned by Ed Swan. The Ohio Power Company bought Swan's business and incorporated it into its location next door. In 1974, this was also razed to make way for the parking lot. Close examination of the photograph below reveals the window of the Ohio Power Company building to the right, which is also visible in the above photograph. (Courtesy of the Rankin family.)

This beautiful house was once the Blazer and Graham Funeral Home, and it was razed to make way for the Ohio Power Company offices. The Ohio Power Company later became American Electric Power, which still uses the back portion as a garage to store supplies. The building has been the location of Light House, a lighting and electrical supplies store, and it currently houses the Ohio Bureau of Motor Vehicles. (Courtesy of Dick Griffin.)

The house at 207 West Main Street was built around 1867 by James P. Cummings, the founder of Cummings Bank and an influential citizen of Carrollton for many years. For the last 76 years, the house has been owned by the Dowell family. The enclosed part of the porch was once part of Drs. Glenn and Charles Dowell's waiting room. Because the trees are so tall, the photograph below was taken from the front instead of the side. (Courtesy of the author.)

This is a view of what was known as Oak Hill and is today West Main Street. The street was paved with bricks made at the Carrollton Paving Brick Company, which was known nationwide for its paving bricks. Streets as far away as New York were once paved with bricks from the Carrollton Paving Brick Company. When roadwork is done, it is still possible to get a glimpse of these bricks, which lie beneath the asphalt of today. (Courtesy of Dick Griffin.)

This house was built by Judge Isaac Taylor in the 1890s in the popular mansion style of that time period. It was best known as the home of George J. Butler, who owned the general store on the square. Butler was also a director of the Cummings Trust Company and a vice president of the Carrollton Electrical Company. Today this house is an apartment building owned by Richard Hannon and John Baker. (Courtesy of the Rankin family.)

The Tastee-Freez was owned by the Best family for many years and was the only fast food restaurant in the area during the 1980s. The building has undergone many face-lifts and business changes during the past decade. It has been Catalina's Mexican restaurant, a pet store, and a Cash Advance. Today it sits empty. (Courtesy of Vickie Nign.)

In 1915, this house at 415 West Main Street was owned by Homer J. Richards, manager of the L&M Rubber Company. The people in the above photograph are believed to be his family. Sadly, this was one of the houses razed to make room for Thorne's Market, and the site on which it once stood is now used for parking. (Courtesy of the Carroll County Historical Society.)

This house was owned by Judge John Fimple, who was a state representative and served as a law clerk under Pres. Benjamin Harrison's administration. The house was later owned by Dr. Ray George. When Thorne's decided to add on to its grocery store, the house was offered to anyone who could move it. Sadly, no one came forward, and the house was razed. Rather than the empty lot that stands in its place today, the house is pictured as it was, photographed by Dr. George Rankin just before its demolition. (Courtesy of the Rankin family.)

This lot was sold on March 27, 1905, for $500. It sits across the street from Thorne's and was purchased by Perry O. McCully in 1908 for $4,500. McCully owned and operated the Carrollton Milling Company, which is now known as the Farmer's Exchange. The house was extensively remodeled by Linda Howell, the current owner. Howell's daughter operates Margi's Dog House pet grooming on the property. (Courtesy of the Rankin family.)

This brick house was built around 1890 for Wallace and Anna (Wathey) Handley, who moved to Carrollton in 1882. The couple married in 1877, and Wallace, a native of Hopedale, Ohio, began a successful law practice in 1881. The house was later purchased by Dr. Glenn C. Dowell, who moved in 1932 when he purchased the J. P. Cummings home on the corner of Main and High Streets. The house is now owned by the McConnaughy family. (Courtesy of the Carroll County Historical Society.)

The house in the background is currently the home of Lynn and Betty Fox. It was built shortly after January 3, 1876, by William Butler. Butler decided he did not want his neighbor, J. P. Cummings, to "look down on him," so he added a cupola. It was removed in 1948, when the house was purchased by the Kempthornes. The building in the foreground of the photograph below is the Carroll Laundromat. (Courtesy of Dick Griffin.)

This building has been many things—gas station, auto repair, another gas station, and arts center—but is still the original construction. Extensive remodeling was done when the building was purchased by the Carroll County Advancement of the Arts Center. An elevator was added to allow visitors access to the second floor art gallery. Various classes and displays are held here throughout the year. (Courtesy of Dick Griffin.)

This is the view of West Main Street from the crosswalk between the Paint and Carpet Center and the Ohio Bureau of Motor Vehicles. The historical photograph (below) was taken around 1910. The upper porch of the building in the foreground has remained the same. The Virginia Restaurant and Lounge is the only other recognizable building still standing. (Courtesy of the Rankin family.)

Westfall's Confectionery was the first ice cream parlor in Carrollton and was located on the northeast corner of Main and High Streets. A photograph of High Street (see page 71) shows the top of this building, and a room with many windows is visible. A music class was once taught there. The location is now the parking lot for the Paint and Carpet Center and B. J. Gray Realty. (Courtesy of Dick Griffin.)

M. V. Courtright had a grocery business in this space before Heiniger's store opened here in 1915. Heiniger's sold many goods in addition to groceries and remained open for many years. Throughout the 1960s and into the mid-1980s, this building was home to C&K shoes. For a short period of time, it was a heating and cooling store, and today it is home to Nanny's Memories, an antique store. (Courtesy of Dick Griffin.)

These photographs were taken approximately 83 years apart from the steps of Widder Hardware (now Bud's Farm Toys). The stores of yesteryear are uncertain. The businesses of 2009 are the Carpet Shop, the Ohio State University extension office, McCort's Family Footwear, and Custom Creations. For many years, Householder's sold electronics where the Ohio state office is now, and Saltsman's Pharmacy was the next store over. (Courtesy of the Rankin family.)

CHAPTER 3

North and South Lisbon Streets

The dividing line between east and west in Carrollton is Lisbon Street. This is a view of South Lisbon Street, which is mainly a residential area and leads to Petersburg, Perrysville, and Harrison County. North Lisbon Street has many churches and leads to Lisbon and Salem. It is also State Route 332 heading south and State Route 9 heading north. (Courtesy of Dan Ries.)

The First United Methodist Church was originally located at 290 West Main Street on the site of Doyle Cable's former home. This brick structure was dedicated in August 1894 and is commonly known as the yellow brick church because of its unusual yellow bricks. The house to its left was built in 1913 and has been used as a parsonage by the church, which owns it. This is the corner of South Lisbon Street and Third Street SE. (Courtesy of Dick Griffin.)

The Carrollton Post Office has had many locations. It once was housed in the building where McFadden's Insurance is today, then moved to North Lisbon Street, where Fair Vision is currently, before moving to its current location on South Lisbon Street. The historical photograph shows the Walsh apartments buildings, which were razed in 1960 to make way for the current post office. (Courtesy of the Rankin family.)

Called the bottom of the square because of the slight grade to the land there, North Lisbon Street truly is at the northern end. The Van Horn building, on the left, was listed on the National Register of Historic Places in 1987 thanks to the efforts of Carl Saltsman. The Ohio Bureau of Support building is on the right, and it was behind that building, in Carrollton's early days, that a bear was shot and then roasted where the First Presbyterian Church is now located. (Courtesy of the Carroll County Genealogical Society.)

These photographs show the approximate location of where Daniel Van Horn's stables stood about 1867. During the 1980s, there was a sporting goods store here and Tiffany's Sub Shop in the foreground area. Those buildings were destroyed by fire, and the Sweeney family constructed the new building in the middle. They maintained a furniture store there until October 2008, when the family retired and the Ashtons' Holiday Shoppe opened. (Courtesy of the Rankin family.)

For 130 years, this was the site of a prominent building in Carrollton. It was originally the Farmer's Hotel, managed by Levi Stemple, and it housed the men who built the current courthouse while they worked. Around 1900, it was converted into a grocery store and operated as such for 50 years. Its last use was as an apartment building before it was razed in 1973 for a parking lot for Peacock Cleaners. (Courtesy the Carroll County Genealogical Society.)

Originally built for the Windsor Evaporated Milk Company in 1936, this building sits across from the fairgrounds on North Lisbon. In 1955, U.S. Plugs purchased it, and in 1957, it was sold to the Evans Pipe Company, which was known internationally for clay sewer pipes. The Evans Pipe Company later converted to plastic and was one of the largest producers of plastic sewer pipe in the world. The building is currently owned by Heritage Plastics, maker of PVC conduit and fittings. (Courtesy of Dick Griffin.)

Before the introduction of automobiles in the early 1900s, store owners banded together to maintain the town roads, raking the dirt to keep them smooth. Today the roads are maintained by village, township, or state road officials. In 1907, the roads were paved with bricks, which still lie under the asphalt. Twelfth Street had not yet been constructed in this 1960s photograph (above). (Courtesy of the Carroll County Genealogical Society.)

The county fair has been a long-standing community event in Carrollton. The first fair was held at the courthouse and was later moved up North Lisbon Street to the McGuire property before moving to its current location in 1868. The original grandstand stood until 1942, when it was destroyed by fire. The present grandstand took several years to build because metal was difficult to come by during World War II. The current grandstand was remodeled in 2008. (Courtesy of the author.)

A view of North Lisbon Street farther north shows several of the houses that still stand there. This row is just before Heritage Plastics and the county fairgrounds. The large house in the foreground once served as a parsonage for Mount Pleasant United Methodist Church. It is now privately owned. The house on the turn is where Anne Green lived, the lady for whom the park was named. Today it is where Hess Auto is located. (Courtesy of the Carroll County Historical Society.)

This site was home to many businesses over the years before it was demolished. At one time, it was a livery stable owned by Fryer and Leggett. It was also a Ford dealership owned by W. M. Giesey and the first site of Myers Tin Shop. It was later razed when Henry Myers moved his tin shop to Main Street. Now it serves as a parking lot for Fair Vision. (Courtesy of the Rankin family.)

Prior to being the public library, this was the Carrollton Post Office. When the post office built a new facility in the 1960s, this became the district library. When it became too small to house all the books and serve the growing need for updated equipment, the library was moved to a new facility on Second Street NE across from the elementary school. This was later the location of a computer store, and today it is the site of Dr. Gregory Fair's optometry business. (Courtesy of the author.)

CHAPTER 4

State Route 43 or Canton Road

This photograph was taken at the ground-breaking ceremony for Our Lady of Mercy Catholic Church. The road winding past the trees in the background of the historical photograph later became State Route 43. Jobes Pharmacy now sits about where the white house is in the historical photograph. (Courtesy of Dick Griffin.)

There is not much to tell about this house, but Dr. George Rankin had the foresight to take a photograph of it. It was a private home for many years but was an apartment around 1985. It was torn down when Advance Auto Parts decided to locate its store on the site. (Courtesy of the Rankin family.)

This beautiful home was owned by the Owen family, and Ellen Owen had a beauty salon there. The house sat on the corner of Canton Road and Crest Street and was razed around 1995 to make way for a Wendy's fast food restaurant. Dr. George Rankin took the older photograph. Behind this property are the Carrollton Crest Apartments and the St. John's Villa facilities. (Courtesy of the Rankin family.)

With its tiled mural, Carrollton Graphics, Inc., was a recognizable local business for many years. Some of the things the business printed were the local *Free Press Standard*, advertisements for many grocery and department stores, newsletters, and Stark Tech College's course listings. The company closed around 2002, and the site was remodeled into the Sherwood Shopping Center. The first store in this location was the Goodwill Store. (Courtesy of Vickie Nign.)

Many residents remember Al's Foodliner, especially its bakery. This IGA was popular, and at one point, it was also called Reed's. Local residents mourned its closure after a fire in the 1980s. After the fire, a portion of the building was able to be used, but it was not the same. It then sat empty for a few years, until the shopping plaza pictured above was opened. This plaza includes Cutler Realty, Custom Cycles, and the Movie Gallery. (Courtesy of Vickie Nign.)

Throughout the 1960s, this was home to Huebner's Chevrolet, which was owned by Archie Huebner. Mr. Cost Plus, Huebner's alter ego, was an icon in Carrollton for many years. Some time between 1967 and 1969, a new facility was built farther north on Canton Road, and when Huebner moved, Scott Cole took over ownership. This building is now home to D&D TV and Appliances, which is owned by Dan Ries. (Courtesy of the Rankin family.)

The Carrollton Exempted Village School District used this site as its bus garage for many years until a new garage was built off of Fifth Street around 1985. Goshen Dairy, an ice cream distributor out of New Philadelphia, Ohio, built an ice cream parlor at this location. For a brief time after Goshen Dairy closed, a business called Smoker's Paradise was located here. Now it is the Rossi Drive-Thru. (Courtesy of the Rankin family.)

The Carroll Electric Cooperative began in 1936, when Pres. Franklin D. Roosevelt introduced the Rural Electrification Administration, designed to help rural customers receive electricity. It is a cooperative, because it is owned by the people who use its services. The cooperative's first office was on the Public Square, and the first lines were energized just before Christmas 1938. By December 1948, the cooperative was moved to this location, where it still provides electric service to Carroll County's rural areas to this day. (Courtesy of the Carroll County Genealogical Society.)

CHAPTER 5

High Street and Beyond

There are so many historical sites in Carrollton that it seems a book could be written for each street, and while this book must come to an end, its story does not. This volume ends with High Street and a few of the side streets around town. This photograph shows High Street looking north. The building to the right was Westfall's Confectionery. (Courtesy of the Rankin family.)

The first train depot in Carrollton was a frame station that was built in 1880 and was torn down in 1912 to make way for the current brick structure. The rail line that passed through carried passengers and items for the Wheeling and Lake Erie railroad for many years. For a brief time, it was used by the Elderberry Excursion Line. Now trains seldom pass through, and the building is used as a restaurant called the Depot Bar and Grill. (Courtesy of Dick Griffin.)

There has been a mill in Carrollton since Isaac Atkinson built the first one on Second Street SE in the early 1800s. That mill changed hands several times, and in 1911, M. V. Courtright teamed with then-owner P. O. McCully to move the mill to the corner of High Street and Second Street NW. Using materials from the old mill, they created what is now known as the Carrollton Farmer's Exchange. (Courtesy of the Rankin family.)

This street scene was taken in front of the Allmon-Dugger-Cotton Funeral Home on Second Street NW facing west. The old standpipe is just visible in the historical photograph between the trees at the end of the street. It is because of that standpipe that the road jogs slightly at the intersection of Second Street and Lincoln Avenue. Because of all the trees, these two photographs do not look very different. (Courtesy of the Carroll County Historical Society.)

The current water tower stands between Garfield and McKinley Avenues. This tower helps supply water to the entire village. Nathan Lane took this wonderful now photograph in the summer of 2008. The original standpipe was about a block away on the corner of Second Street NW (then North Street) and Lincoln Avenue. (Courtesy of Dan Ries.)

The photograph below is of Carrollton Pottery, of which nothing remains except the empty lot seen in the above photograph. Beside it was the Carrollton Manufacturing Company, which began in 1898 as a foundry and later became the Hosterman Novelty Works, manufacturing toys and miscellaneous small metal products. Around 1931, it became Carrollton Metal Products, which mainly produced stainless steel cookware. In the late 1970s, the company sold the buildings to Fusion Ceramics, which still uses them today. (Courtesy of Dan Ries.)

The Landmark Store that once sat here was a farm supply store organized by the Carroll County Farm Bureau Co-Op around 1948. The first meeting of the farm bureau was in 1919 and operated under the supervision of the cooperative extension work of the U.S. Department of Agriculture. The organization became a co-op on June 9, 1948, and the store was established for the convenience of its members. It was located on North High Street until the 1990s. (Courtesy of Dick Griffin.)

Probate court judge J. C. Ferrall was the first owner of this house, which sits on the corner of Second Street SW and High Street. He also owned a general store and, in 1884, was a presidential elector for the Democratic ticket. Dr. Carl Lincke later purchased the house and sided it in stone. It is now owned by Lincke's daughter Ann and her husband, Carl Saltsman, who owned Saltsman's Pharmacy. (Courtesy of the Carroll County Historical Society.)

Located at 239 High Street NW, this building was originally constructed by the Farmer's Exchange and used for its lumber sales and storage. When the Lumber Service built a new facility on Trump Road, this building was remodeled, and Light House took it over and still uses it today. (Courtesy of Vickie Nign.)

This house was built in 1870 by Robert Atkinson. In 1890, half of the lot was given up so the town could build High Street. The house sat empty for many years until 1939, when it was purchased by George C. Rankin. It changed hands a couple of times after Rankin's death and was purchased by National City Bank in the early 1980s. Now it is the location of the Allstate Insurance office run by Tom Turnipseed. (Courtesy of the Rankin family.)

The house that sat next door to the Atkinson property was purchased from Lee Stafford and razed in 1976 by Banc Ohio, a division of the National City Bank in Cleveland. The bank had used a drive-through on the other side of the Atkinson house but decided to replace it with this one. The drive-through is still used by National City Bank today. The previous drive-through was enclosed and is now an office. (Courtesy of the Rankin family.)

The General Telephone Company of Ohio constructed this building when it switched to the dial telephone system from a battery-operated telephone system where an operator dialed the desired number for a caller. That also marked the switch from five- to seven-digit telephone numbers, which changed in the 1990s, when a 10-digit number was required. Verizon now uses the building to serve its telephone and Internet customers. (Courtesy of the author.)

County treasurer Joseph G. Kennedy constructed the original building for the village fire department. In 1948, that house was demolished and a new city building was constructed. In 1991, a new fire and police station called the Safety Center was built, and this became the Municipal Building. The Municipal Building houses the mayor's office, and citizens can pay water bills and local taxes there. (Courtesy of the author.)

The first fire department was organized in the 1860s as an all-volunteer service. In 1936, it was reorganized into the Carrollton Village Fire Department. The county volunteer department resides on Kensington Road. The current village department is located on Third Street SW and also houses the village police department. A firemen's frolic is held once a year to help support the village fire department. (Courtesy of the Rankin family.)

Ed Long has been selling tractors and parts for at least 40 years. The Ohio Bureau of Motor Vehicles used the parallel parking space in front of his store to test new drivers until the early 1990s. An annual gathering of folks who remember Coley's Stag restaurant from Main Street is held here, usually in November. (Courtesy of Vickie Nign.)

William H. Harrison was a probate judge from Harrison County. When he retired from the courtroom, he came to Carrollton and practiced law for 18 years. His home was on Second Street SE across from the courthouse and jail. The house was torn down and is now employee parking for the courthouse. The cement stairs leading up from Second Street are the only thing that remains of this home. (Courtesy of the Rankin family.)

What is known as the top of Public Square is really the southern end. This house is located next to the old J. C. Penney store and is now used as apartments. The photograph below is dated 1949. Some of the old aerial photographs taken around 1913 also show this same house. The most remarkable thing about these photographs is the difference in the land. Notice the parking meter at the top. (Courtesy of the Rankin family.)

Some time after 1988, the First United Methodist Church purchased this house and razed it for additional parking. Until that time, the house had been owned by the Dunlap family. The corner of the church and the garage can be seen in both photographs. (Courtesy of the Rankin family.)

Third Street SE was originally called Liberty Street. This is the intersection with South Lisbon Street. Many prominent founding citizens lived on this street. It was also the site of the first automobile ride in Carrollton, which took place around 1905. The large house in the background has a third floor big enough that when the circus came to town, the troop would practice there. Until the early 1990s, trapeze ropes still hung from its rafters. (Courtesy of Dan Ries.)

This house was built in 1834 by Judge William Johnson with bricks burned on the premises. These proved to be too soft, and the house was then covered with redwood siding. The house was later purchased by Gen. Ephraim Eckley, who was the last living congressman to serve under Pres. Abraham Lincoln. Pres. William McKinley and his wife, Ida Saxton McKinley, were once guests of General Eckley's. Today the house is owned by Gene and Julie Shuman. (Courtesy of the Rankin family.)

In 1913, the *Carroll Chronicle* called this house, located on the corner of Fourth Street SE and Ray Avenue, one of the best houses in Carrollton. Dan Getzman sold the house to Virge Stoody, an embalmer and undertaker from Dellroy, when Stoody was elected in 1913 as the county auditor. At that time the street was called Prospect Street. (Courtesy of the author.)

Around 1915, this house was home to the family of Thomas J. Saltsman, a banker for the Cummings Bank. It is now the location of Judge Charles Johnston's law office on Second Street NE, next to the public library. After a severe storm, the upper floor of the home had to be removed. Judge Johnston had the new roof made to resemble the original as much as possible. (Courtesy of the Rankin family.)

This was the home of Jacob Helfrich and his large family. It was built in the 1840s, and members of the Helfrich family lived here until the 1930s. In 1900, Jacob Helfrich became the owner of a shoe store on the square that bore his name. His son, John W., later used the building for a jewelry store and was known for his clocks. The house was purchased by Dr. Carl Lincke in the 1940s and was converted into several apartments. (Courtesy of the Carroll County Genealogical Society.)

When the construction of this building took longer than expected, students attended classes in several nearby buildings. It was built to house grades 1–12, and when it was completed in 1913, people believed it was too big and would never be filled. Just five short years later, the building was overflowing, and plans for a second building began. Today this building houses kindergarten through fourth grade. (Courtesy of Dan Ries.)

To accommodate increased student enrollment, this building opened in 1927 as a high school and served as such until 1955, when additional space was needed. A new high school was then constructed behind the elementary school, and this building became the Bell-Herron Middle School, which houses grades six through eight. The fifth grade is taught in a wing of the high school. (Courtesy of Dan Ries.)